Tips from a Mediator

for divorcing couples

Lynley Barnett

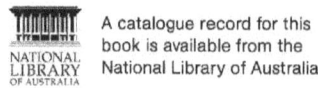
A catalogue record for this book is available from the National Library of Australia

Text Copyright © 2023 Lynley Barnett
Illustration Copyright © 2023 Helen Iles
All rights reserved.
ISBN-13: 978-1-922727-96-1

Linellen Press
265 Boomerang Road
Oldbury, Western Australia
www.linellenpress.com.au

Dedication

To all the divorcing couples who just need a few survival tips to help them through a difficult time in their lives.

Firstly, my sympathy. Secondly, my tips as a retired mediator.

Foreword

When couples are committed to separation and divorce, they are often in a great deal of pain.

While they are in this state, they are being asked to make decisions related to children, and to property.

It is an extremely difficult time.

Mediators know this.

However, the Family Court does require that, if couples were in a married or in a defacto relationship, there is a time limit in applying to finalise property. You need to check this out so that you have the information that applies to your circumstances.

Couples may use Mediation, DIY, or legal assistance in creating Parenting Plans and Property Disposal.

If you wish to take your documents to Court and register them when completed then mediation is a prerequisite for parenting plans.

The Mediators' Motto for separating couples is this:

"They're doing the best they can."

So, for some, it will take weeks to arrive at a Parenting Plan, and weeks to divide property.

But don't think mediation won't work because of distance, or the hurt feelings between you. Mediation can be done:

- face to face;
- between two separate rooms;
- one person on a phone;
- two persons on a phone;
- zoom appointments;
- between states; between countries.

Communication and technology can bring people together in many different ways. You just have to get the actual timing right.

Mediation can be done with a translator present.

Mediation can be done with a lawyer available, usually by phone, or in a separate room to answer questions. But remember they have to be paid too.

There is a cooperative principle:

Give a little to get a little.
Generosity begets generosity.

Using Mediation Services for both Parenting plans and Property division is usually a less expensive way for couples. Not all Mediation Services offer both, so check this out.

It is never going to be satisfactory for both parties. No one likes to "share" their children. Nor do they like to see all their hard-earned savings and property "divided."

So, let's acknowledge this right at the beginning.

No one ever said separating or divorcing would be easy.

What follows are some tips that might make it less of a personal and painful experience.

Notes on Parenting Plans and Property Disposal

Parenting plans are made to allow both parents to arrive at how their children will spend time with each parent, and how they will be parented into the future.

Property Disposal is dividing up your property in such a way that neither party is disadvantaged.

The following tips are suggested for your Parenting Plan, and for the disposal of Property.

It may be that later, as your relationship becomes calmer, you can once again trust each other and verbal agreements can be made but, at the commencement of this distressing time, it is better to have things in writing, not because either party cannot be trusted, but because you forget what you say when you are angry and distressed.

You may read on and say "common sense".

And I agree, much of what I have written in this book is "Common Sense" – the only problem is that it is not so common.

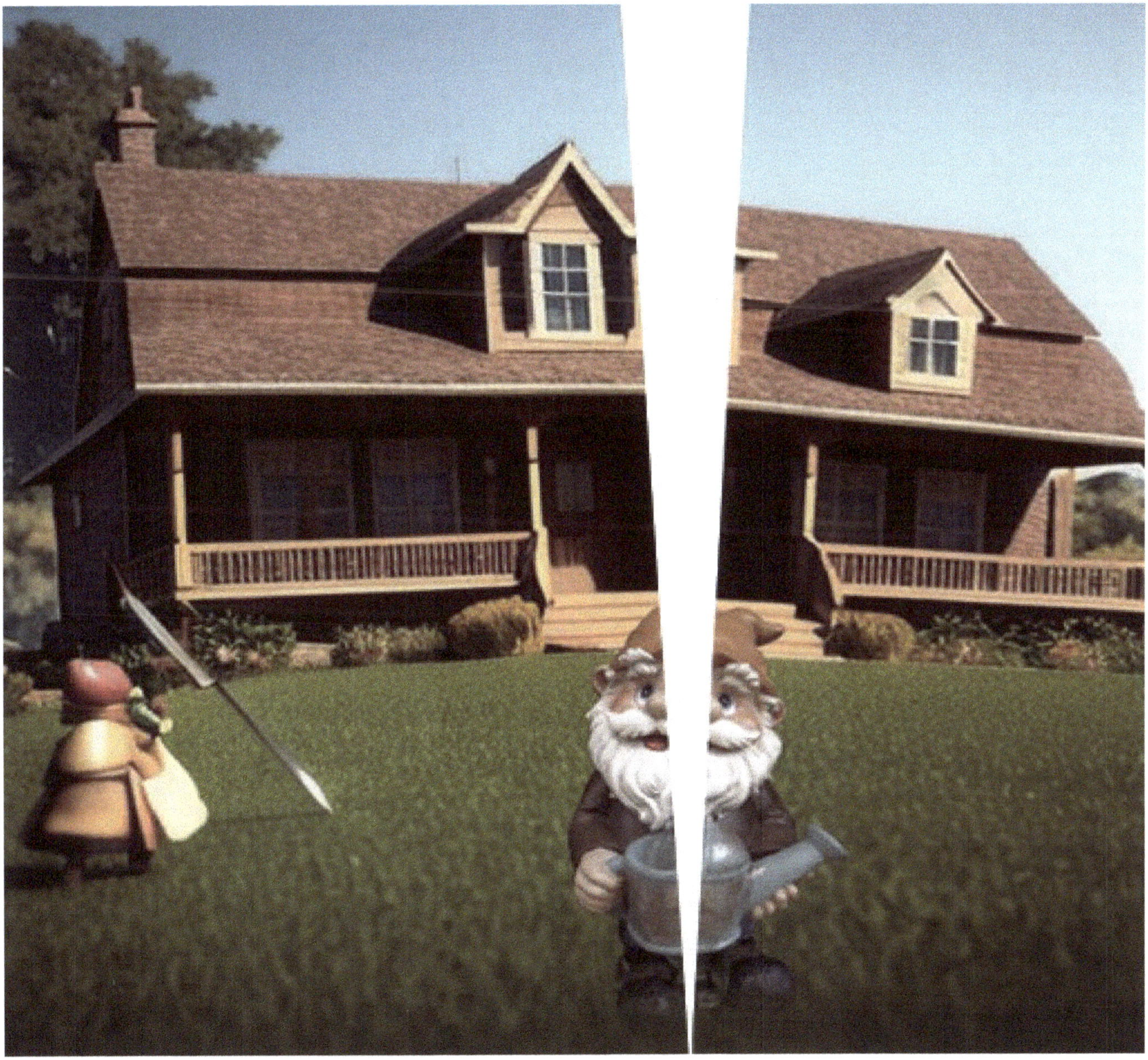

Tip number one.

Getting started.

Always commence your parenting plans by using respectful phrases. You might say: Mary Smith and Fred Smith have created a Parenting Plan for their children, Susan aged 10, and Thomas aged 8. Their wish is to ensure both children spend time with each parent and enjoy the company and benefits each parent may give to the children.

And mean it.

If you learn to use respectfulness throughout your deliberations you can diminish antagonism and hostility.

Tip number two

Reviews

When writing up your parenting plan include the clause that says: "This parenting plan will be reviewed at the commencement of each year. Both parents commit to a time to review the plan and to make amendments as needed. If they are unable to do this amicably between themselves, they will use a mediator or a third party."

Think about this. Children grow up. Their needs change. Their wants multiply. And what they want this week they may not want next week: they are, after all, children.

And parents' circumstances change. A FIFO (Fly-in-Fly-out) worker may decide to work in town. An ex may decide to return to TAFE or Uni. All of this creates the need to amend plans.

So, Common sense says: 'Review arrangements regarding the children'.

Tip number three

Changes

If parents can come to an amicable decision between themselves regarding changes to the parenting plans in existence, they should write these down, copy and share them, sign and date them.

If you want them legally recognised, put the amendments through the Courts.

Tip number four

Emails/Texts

Keep all emails that go between you.
Print them and file them under date and year.
You can do the same with texts.
There will come a day when you can bin the lot, but until that day arrives this little piece of housekeeping will save you time and energy.

Tip number five

Correspondence.

Keep all other correspondence that goes between you.
And keep your files separate. That is: Parenting is one file. Property is another file.
Make sure everything is dated.

Tip number six

Copies.

Keep a copy of anything you write that is related to parenting plans or property.

Don't post anything without having a copy in your possession.

Simply, don't trust your memory.

Tip number seven

Choose how you view things

Don't think of the above as being something grim and unpleasant, rather think of it as you being organised.

You'll be eternally grateful many times over that you have kept a record.

Trust me it makes it easier for you.

Tip number eight

Being practical

The overriding thought when making decisions about where children will live is

'WHAT is in the best interests of the children?'

And this will change as they grow older. Be prepared to acknowledge that, and to allow for that in your discussions.

So, for love of the children, be practical.

Very little children need the consistency of one parent. That will evolve as the child grows and goes to Kindy and school.

It has nothing to do with who loves the child the most. Nor who is the better cook.

But, if one parent is a FIFO worker, it most certainly has a huge bearing on maintaining the relationship of the children with that parent.

Tip number nine.

"Away" parents

Addressing all FIFO workers, or any parent who works out of town for periods of time, like members of the Defence Forces:

How will you maintain your good relationship with your children?

If the children do not have their own phones one can be bought which is used perhaps every night at 7 pm to speak face to face to the away parent.

Each child has their time with the away parent.

Any time variation of this can be agreed on.

And for the at-home parent, this is your time to allow privacy for those conversations to be held, away from your ears. You want your children to grow up knowing what respect is and this is a way of role-modelling it.

And whatever you do ...! don't let that contact with the other parent be used as a privilege to be removed if a child misbehaves. It isn't a privilege! It is a right!

It is acknowledged that some away parents may be unable to make contact on a regular pattern with their children. So this is when that parent gets creative.

Arrange for small parcels to be posted to the children.

Or funny letters.

Write them in advance. Cover them in stickers.

Think of the Dad who sent furniture for the Dolls' house, one item at a time for weeks and weeks. Clever man.

Or the smart Army parent who organised stickers and fairy dust to be sent to the Fairy-mad daughter.

Buy cards or postcards at every port you go into; send them to the children.

A travel tour with the away parent. It's like learning secondhand about the Countries of the World.

Take a picture of yourself in every port and sent that with a text message.

Look, your children may think you are raving mad, but they will also enjoy that you think of them, and you show it.

Get the Grandparents to help execute your creativity. Especially if you have to miss a birthday. Deputise Grandparents to take your present to the child whose birthday you will miss.

But, do it. Stay in contact.

All children need a constant reminder from you that they are loved.

Tip number ten

School holidays

Some parents just halve the holidays, so that the children spend an equal amount of time with each parent.

Some organise time with grandparents as well. (More about grandparents later.)

And what if one parent wants to take the children on a camping trip and cannot get back at exactly the right time for equal sharing of the holidays?

Let me introduce you to Mr and Mrs Common Sense.

Give a little. That way you will be able to ask for a little if something special comes up, like "Disney on Ice", or tickets to the Grand Final and you want to take the children with you.

Tip number eleven

Changeovers

Picking up the children is often done better when there isn't contact with the other parent.

So, it looks like this: Parent A picks the children up from school on a Friday every week, or every second week. He or she returns them to school on the Monday.

Parent B collects them from school on Monday and has the children until the Friday.

Public Holidays occur often on a Monday. This needs discussion.

Who will have them? Get creative. Maybe one parent has ALL Public Holidays throughout the year, and in exchange, the other parent has an extra week at Christmas time?

Maybe it gets called Grandparent Day and they get to see Grandparents on the Public Holidays. Everyone knows where they stand when the picture is as clear as this.

Tip number twelve

Children's Birthdays, Parent's Birthdays

This is something that should be plain and straightforward.

Parent A has the children for their birthdays in the first year, Parent B has the Children for their birthdays in Year 2.

That means that in the first year, if there are to be parties, Parent A is responsible for them. The following year, Parent B is responsible for the parties.

It is that simple: it alternates each year. And those parties or that birthday may be celebrated on a weekend because of the difficulty with schooling.

Hullo, Mr and Mrs Common Sense. Sure, you may have to lose a day on a weekend, but just maybe that can be replaced by those Monday Public Holidays. See above, get creative.

If you can invite the other parent to the party, good for you. If you cannot, make sure they have all the information about the party so that they can discuss the party with the child. Remember it is THEIR special day. Your feelings would be better put to one side for that day.

Does it stop you from having two cakes? Or the Grandparents coming over for tea?

Of course not, but a party with children's friends on two separate weekends by two separate parents lacks Common Sense. As the parents of the invited children will tell you, which party do they attend?

Dad and Mum's birthdays? Arrange with the children how you will celebrate your birthday with them. Make it another fabulous occasion. Go boating, fishing, picnicking, hire some bikes — think outside the box.

Tip number thirteen

Christmas Day.

This is something that often gets done badly. So let's make it simple.

Parent A has the children from Christmas Eve Day and ALL Christmas Day. Two nights.

Parent B has the Children from all Boxing Day and the following day, and they return the day after. Two nights.

Every year thereafter, this alternates. Each parent gets the children for all of Christmas Day, without opening presents gobbling dinner, then rewrapping presents and being rushed off to the next place for another Christmas meal and more opening of presents.

But suit yourself here; just ask yourself, who are you doing this for: you, or the children?

Ask yourself: How would you like to be rushed here there and everywhere on Christmas Day? Just saying.

Where there are other religions, the same principles apply. Upholding the Rituals of their religion will be shared. The sharing is done by compromise or alternating yearly with each parent.

The objective here is that the inclusion of the children is done without fuss, and with anticipation of the fun they will have.

Tip number fourteen

Get creative

ONE: Children do not have to be entertained. You would not have done this when you were still together. But you do have to think outside the box.

Could you teach your child Chess?

Could you teach your child Solitaire?

Could you teach them to paint?

How to keep a scrapbook

It occupies their time, and it's fun. Know any courses that they might like to be enrolled in, like a day with the Soccer players? A tennis camp? A cooking Class? You are a parent; now it is up to you to know their interests and encourage them.

Think outside the box: Some of your best resources may be other parents.

Get creative TWO: Make up a book that tells the child/children what decisions you two have made regarding the time they spend with each parent. Make it a project you do together; make it fun. Fill it with pictures. Make it into a Fun Diary which gets updated as needed.

Get Creative THREE: Get the children to look forward to time with you, Dad, or Mum. Plan something for "next" time. A baking afternoon? A bike ride? Going to the footy, basketball?

But, do not let them down. Fulfil your promises.

Tip number fifteen

Choosing a school

If you have a desire for your children to attend certain schools, you are going to need to navigate this with the other parent.

It may be that proximity means that they attend School xyz.

If this becomes a major hurdle on which you cannot reach an agreement, you may choose to take this one difficulty before the family court to be resolved.

On the other hand, you may want to leave them exactly where they are now to keep them settled, and leave the school decisions until the following year.

And do the children get a say in this?

That depends on their age and maturity.

Tip number sixteen

Music, Sport, Hobbies

What did you want your children to be involved in before you broke up? So, what's changed? Can they still continue with the sport, music or hobby?

And if not why not?

Go carefully here because your children are going to want an explanation that they can understand. And being "ticked off" with Parent B is not a good enough reason to refuse the children to be in a sport.

Whatever gets decided write this into the plan, but be aware that it could change due to financial circumstances

Tip number seventeen

Children's Health

You need to make sure you write into a Parenting Plan that whoever has responsibility for the children will also be responsible for their health needs, for the period of time that they are with them.

This means:

One: that you keep all medications likely to be needed at both residences.

Two: that you both have access to the Doctors used for the children, and

Three: that should any emergency occur, the other parent will be fully informed as soon as practicable.

So, who keeps the records of the children's medical visits and inoculations?

Both parents. Use a photocopier or a shared app that stores the children's data, where everyone can access it.

If a child is on medication that should travel between homes, then both parents should be aware of all the circumstances for which this medication is needed; how it must be taken, and when, are simple practicalities.

Some children have medical problems that are either hereditary or acquired. The information about medicines, treatment in emergencies, and telephone numbers to ring in emergencies must be kept by both parents, and all other family members need an understanding of the basic care essential for this child.

Remember, children forget. Write the information needed for such an emergency and paste it on the back of a cupboard door that can be reached by all.

Tip number eighteen

Notes re the children

Some parents use a booklet that goes between parents. In it, they say "Fred has a Dr's apt on Saturday at 10am. This was the only time Dr Black was free. Attached is his card." This assumes that Parent B knows what the illness is; Common Sense assumes you have told the parent.

Or "The Junior Basketball on Sunday is cancelled due to the weather forecast."

Or "Simon Says has a Birthday on Monday evening. All the children are meeting at Chicken Treat at 6 pm. Here is the invitation."

It contains only information about the children, or directly related to the children. It is never used to berate the other parent. Not one word is entered into this booklet which could make a child distressed.

Tip number nineteen

Grandparents

Grandparents have a huge role to play in children's growth and development. The saying is that it takes "a community to raise a child." That community includes aunties and uncles, cousins, friends and grandparents.

Many people write into a Parenting Plan that it is acceptable for either of the grandparents to have the children. They just have to negotiate times and days with the parent who has them at that time. Remember, it is only you two who are getting divorced, not all the relatives. And why on earth would you deprive your children of relatives who love the children?

And do you think grandparents should only have them on their son's time, or their daughter's time? Use Mr and Mrs Common Sense. If the fair is on this weekend and *either* set of grandparents has the energy to take the grandchildren, wing a prayer of thanks upstairs.

Tip number twenty

So you want to take the children overseas.

This has to be carefully negotiated. Which countries? And why?

Consider asking questions about health in those countries. Consider asking who will be looking after the children.

If you are going to write this into a Parenting Plan, do it in such a way that it says both parents will discuss this, and no child will be taken out of the country on holiday without the other parent's written permission.

Consider whether you want your children to go to other states on holiday; maybe that also gets written in as not without prior permission from both parents.

And who holds the passports? Sometimes it is neither parent, but the Court or a trusted person instead.

Tip number twenty-one

Property

When it comes to property being dissolved, your motto should be like the Boy Scouts' motto: "Be Prepared".

You will need a copy of all the documents related to property. And you will need to make a list of:

- house ownership,
- mortgage repayments,
- bank account statements,
- shares,
- superannuation,
- incomes,
- chattels, (that's the furniture and all items within the house.)
- Cars,
- Caravans,
- trailers,
- tools.

If you have something that is owned, it comes to the table to be discussed. But don't get frightened by the seemingly endless list.

You will need to get appraisals of what the items are worth, at least the major items. But you can agree on what the minor items are worth.

And here's what you need to know: You need to reach an agreement on the value of your items, and then items can be shared or disposed of.

You don't get to change the value each week. You settle on a value and then work with that. That includes shares, which tend to rise and fall.

You can go through kitchen items one by one and that would end up taking you about a year to agree on the value of each item, so usually you accept a collective amount for the lot.

Sometimes one parent or the other wants a specific item, so it is usual for the minor item to be declared as:

Mary will keep the refrigerator valued at, and Tom will keep the Trailer valued at. Or if your grandmother's Dining Set is something you have a sentimental yearning for you, ask for that with its agreed value being abc.

So how to simplify this?

Make your list of what you would like from the chattels. This can then be negotiated if there are one or two items that each might want. A monetary value figure can be put on each list. Then you are left with the house, the car, the supers, and maybe a caravan. Who wants what? Who needs what?

Make sure you understand the Superannuation laws as they relate to you.

Incomes and Businesses are discussed as well, so be prepared for all details to be made accessible to both parents.

It is usual for the property division to be made on percentages. Like 60% to one and 40% to the other. What goes into that percentage could be anything jointly owned, or separately owned. And it is completely natural to negotiate the golf clubs for the vacuum cleaner. This is a settlement that needs to work for both of you.

Think about how long the marriage or partnership has lasted, and what finances or property were brought into the relationship, and how many children there are from this relationship. That is all relevant to a division of property.

And then there is the parent who worked for wages and the parent who worked without getting paid a wage. That, of course, refers to the parent who stayed home and created a home and raised the children.

If it all sounds like it's too much, just trust your mediator or lawyer. He or she has probably written hundreds of property divisions. They will guide you through each step of a property division.

If the worst comes to the worst and you cannot agree on anything, that is what the Family Court is for. Unfortunately, the only drawback here is that there will be a time lapse before you get your day in court.

Tip number twenty-two

The Family Court

Family Courts are there for the protection of children, and for fairness in separation and divorce. They have experienced Judges on the Bench and staff who are trained in mediation. And they are people who have seen it all – the good, the bad, and the ugly.

Don't even think you can fool them.

If you want to sit in on a Family Court while it is in Session, ask permission and then follow the court's proceedings. It may make you work harder at a solution between you both.

Tip number twenty-three

Children's Black Board/White Board/Calendar.

Children forget things. They forget clothes. They forget appointments. Just take a look at the Lost and Found Boxes that most schools have. It is full of left behind items. It's why you learn to mark all school items and every piece of clothing they wear to school.

So do something equally as sensible. Have a whiteboard or a blackboard somewhere central for the child. On it write "You have a Birthday party to attend on Saturday. When will we get the present for Fred?" Or "All clothes from Soccer need to be out in the laundry by tomorrow evening." Teach them to take responsibility for their sports clothing, books, and homework.

Sometimes the messages might just be "Love you. Have a good day!"

Common Sense would tell you this: Children forget but they can read. And this is a lot better than nagging.

Tip number twenty-four

Homework

This can be tricky. Getting homework done when children go between two homes is not always easy.

This way of dealing with Homework originated between two parents with several children. They had a Homework time set aside for all children collectively, no matter which house the children resided in.

Friday night was Homework free; Saturday night was Homework-free, but Sunday the Homework time rule applied – unless they were lucky enough to have none set for that weekend.

Write this into a Parenting Plan if it helps both of you manage the children in a similar manner.

Children like routine. It is comforting, and makes them feel safe. They know what is expected of them.

Tip number twenty-five

Telling the teachers

Schools and the children's teachers need to be made aware of the separation.

They need to know who drops off the children and who will pick them up after school.

Or the bus numbers and routes that these children will take.

If anything changes, the class teacher needs a polite note given to the teacher. Where grandparents are involved, the teachers need to be aware of this also.

Mr and Mrs Common Sense are telling you what? Yes, that's right. They are telling you that **Safety for Children is a priority!**

Tip number twenty-six

Technology

The dreaded phones and iPads/tablets and time spent on them.

If you didn't have a set of rules jointly decided on before the separation, it will be difficult to create a set of rules now. Not impossible but difficult. You absolutely do need to do this cooperatively, for everyone's sake.

You could have a small broadsheet with children's names down the side, and across the top the days of the week.

How many hours on each piece of technology are they allowed? May they have more hours on the weekend? Do Nana and Pop have to adhere to these rules? Are the hours age-related? E.g. teenager v primary-age child.

What constitutes an emergency when the rules may be broken?

Happy days. It isn't easy getting accord on this one, but as near as you both can make it easier for the children.

And if they break the rules, then I guess they lose time on the piece. But both of you need to be in agreement with this too, for all your sakes.

Remember this: you are not separating or divorcing your children. You are still Mum and/or Dad. Your parenting ideas need to be as similar as possible. And try to make them simple enough for all children to understand.

Simple enough for them to realise that you are still a part of their life, even though you meet together less often.

Tip number twenty-seven

Pocket Money

If you have paid your children for doing chores, then it makes sense to continue doing that.

If you give your children an allowance each week, why stop? Mum and Dad, you both need to agree on the allowance that each child receives, and who is responsible for giving it to the children.

And if you want to give your children a head-start in managing money, the Barefoot Investor has written a book for children. Teaching your children how to manage money may be one of the most valuable lessons you will give them.

Tip number twenty-eight

Use off-sets

If Parent A buys two sets of school clothes, one for each home, perhaps Parent B could be responsible for buying the iPad or Tablet needed for school work.

Trade, negotiate. Bargain fairly.

And there is nothing wrong with keeping one second-hand set of school clothes at each house – that's for when the children leave something behind, which they will do sooner or later.

Children do have so many things on their minds that they forget some pretty basic things.

Tip number twenty-nine

One Up-manship

You play One up-manship at your peril

Trying to outdo the other parent to win a child's favour teaches children how to manipulate.

Children are quick learners. They become very adept at manipulating parents, and once you have started this, expect it for the rest of your life. Remember, you *have* been warned.

General

Nothing is easy about separating and divorce; remember I said that at the beginning.

Regardless of why your separation came about, here are two adults who can show a willingness to be caring of their children.

And, a willingness to divide their property fairly.

You care; you give a little, and you get a little, and you maintain a relationship with both your partner and your children.

And before I forget:

Children are not mini-adults. Their concepts are developing as they grow.

They are not your best friends, nor should they be.

They look to you for adult guidance, and adult care and protection.

Your job is to set boundaries to help them.

If you want a mate, go to the pub and have a drink with one. Children are on loan for you to love and develop.

Now, really, is all this too much to ask from you both?

Other books by Lynley Barnett

Letters from Nana

The Spectacular Cat

Peter's Story

Sophie's Story

Zac's Story

Tomas's Story

About the Author

Lynley Barnett spent many years working in Perth WA as an Alternate Dispute Resolution Practitioner (A.D.R.P.) or, in your words, a Mediator. She worked thousands of hours in Mediation, with adults, couples and businesses. She was appointed an Approved Court Mediator by the Family Court of WA and taught the Attorney Generals Mediation qualifications in Perth.

www.ingramcontent.com/pod-product-compliance
Lightning Source LLC
Chambersburg PA
CBHW051349110526
44591CB00025B/2948